Improve Your Life in 80 Days

DOE ZANTAMATA

DEDICATION

For you.

ABOUT THIS BOOK

This book began as daily messages entitled,
"Days Left of 2018."

It's not meant to be read in one sitting, but rather one page
per day for 80 days. After the 80 days, it can be read again
from the beginning, or kept on a nightstand and a random
page chosen each day.

Through the use and self-work described in this book, you
will gain a deeper understanding of yourself and the world
around you.

How deep you dive will determine how high you rise.

May all of your best dreams come true.

With love and sincere appreciation,

Doe

DAY-01

Today, look in the mirror and thank your body. It's been with you since the day you were born. It's grown, changed, and taken your soul to all the places you've been...from the most difficult to the most amazing. It's been bruised, scraped, wounded, and healed the best it could. Love this vessel from here on out.

DAY-02

Today, take a moment to reflect on this year. How it started, who has left your life, who has entered, who has taken a more distant role, and who has become closer. The ones who have come closer...make a point today to tell them (face to face if possible) how much you appreciate them. Yes, they probably already know but tell them from this reflective place in your mind.

DAY-03

Today, start to believe in yourself. Create confidence by detaching from your old story. When faced with a choice that requires confidence, pause and think of what you would advise your grown up child or someone else who you really love to do. Do that. Or, think of someone you know who you see as both kind and confident. What would they do? Do that. Don't let the "buts" of your old story interrupt you. Make the confident choice.

DAY-04

Today, try something new. Adventure doesn't have to mean skydiving or climbing Mount Everest. Adventure means doing something you haven't done before. Visit a park nearby that you haven't been to yet. Or find a recipe or a restaurant out of your normal food range. Do a yoga video on YouTube or rearrange your furniture. Whether you love it or don't care for it, you've still expanded your mind and opened up a pathway in your mind that says, "things can be different." This pathway will increase the more that you use it, and I guarantee you, it will serve you well.

DAY-05

Today, laugh. Yes, the world is serious and yes, there are a lot of enormous problems that need to be solved, but holding tension in your body won't solve a single one of them. Good hearted laughter at no one's expense breaks up tense energy and floods your mind with positive neurotransmitters. Read some dumb jokes, watch a funny movie, relive some funny stories with friends or family. This puts you in a better frame of mind. In a better frame of mind, you can more easily see how you can resolve or help to resolve problems in a positive way, become motivated to contribute your part, and you can tell what's actually not a problem at all.

DAY-06

Today, flip the switch from lack to abundance. We see what we focus on. We see what we believe in. It's a normal reaction to start worrying when you don't seem to have enough; time, money, patience...whatever it is. But you don't have to travel down that road. Start the day with the mantra: " All that I need, I already have...and more." And any time during the day that you're faced with lack, take a deep breath and repeat it again. It's going to switch your belief and your focus. And you will start to see opportunities that you otherwise would have missed. It sounds too easy to be true, but it works. I promise you, it works. And when the good comes in, don't push it away with disbelief. Receive it, welcome it, with gratitude.

DAY-07

Today, simplify. Starting can get overwhelming really quickly. But life has a habit of letting things collect over time, and freeing up space will lift you of burdens you didn't even realize you were carrying. It may be cleaning out a closet or a drawer, or canceling subscriptions that seemed like a good idea at the time but you really don't want or use them. Start small and feel the good feeling of the stagnant energy opening up and flowing.

This will motivate you to do more. There can be a little guilt involved as you let go of things that you spent money on, but facing that will also create an awareness in you to consider more in the future what you really want and need versus what would be an impulse buy.

DAY-08

Today, step out of your comfort zone. Pretty much everyone is bad at things that require skill or practice when they first start. Whether it's singing, painting, writing, learning a new language, or how to play an instrument. Unless you're unusually talented, you'll likely not be very good on day one. But you know what? Day two you'll be better. Day 47 you'll be a lot better...and by day 1000 you'll be a pro. What's something you've always wanted to do but haven't tried? If you'd started years ago, think how good you'd be by now. But when you start now, think how good you'll be in a few years. Stop ignoring what could be one of the great passions of this beautiful life of yours. Start today.

DAY-09

Today, breathe. You don't own all the problems of the world. It's hard not to get sucked into chaos and of course you want to be aware and do your part, but too much of it can leave you feeling disempowered and in despair. So take a break. Breathe. Breathe ten deep breaths. Feel your center, release the tension you've been holding and have only let go during sleep. Breathe. Three short breaths in and one long, slow one out. Repeat. Come back to you. Break the pattern of getting latched into and whipped around by drama. Choose when you are going to respond and how. Breathe.

DAY-10

Today, live the life of your dreams. If actually believing you can live the life of your dreams is too much of a stretch right now, just stop believing so much that you can't. Start by remembering what those dreams were and evaluate if what was stopping you before is still stopping you now. Times have changed. You have changed. Think about this: what would you do if you had $5 million dollars and 2 years of no commitments? After the vacations, giving money to loved ones, and buying stuff. Your answer is your dream. Now scale that down to an hour a week and what you can do with little or no money and do it. Start living the life of your dreams right now.

DAY-11

Today, stretch. Stretch your body; arms, legs, full body, even your fingers and toes. Stretch your mind: watch a documentary or a how-to video and learn something new, even if you never "use" it. Stretch your heart: pause as you encounter everyone you love who is in your life today. Pause and consciously think of how much you love and appreciate them...this includes pets and this includes you. This is life, the good stuff. We learn, we grow, we love.

DAY-12

Today, practice awareness. That's really just a fancy way of saying stay in the exact moment you're in as much as you can. Our thoughts when left to run amok can bounce around from the past, distant past, future, and what happens is we miss what's happening now. A meal is much more enjoyable when you're paying attention to the good food in front of you and the good person across from you rather than reliving a crummy day at work. Reflecting is often a necessary part of problem solving, sure, but make sure to enjoy your good moments while you're living them in real time. Moments pass by so fast. Don't miss your chance to experience them fully.

DAY-13

Today, start to recognize everything as sacred. Yourself, the people who you come into contact with, your job, the food you prepare and eat, the clothes you wear, your home, even the act of cleaning. Life has the meaning that we give it. That's a choice. A person can see life as meaningless and it will surely become so, or a person can see life as a battle and they will find one everywhere they go. You can choose to see life as sacred, every moment a chance to bring purpose, gratitude, and even joy to everything you do and everyone you meet. Sounds hokey? It's not. It's a habit that can be cultivated and developed and it will literally transform your life.

DAY-14

Today, rekindle. Did you used to make time to do something you really liked, just for you? Maybe it was drawing, or writing, or reading about or tinkering with something that time and life got too busy to keep up with. Well, times have changed. One of the positive things about how fast paced technology has become is that some things that were expensive or time consuming before have now become very inexpensive and many times even free. Rekindle that spark in you that wanted to learn, or dream, or create, or ever wondered about doing any of those things. You can do more in a half hour now than what you could before in a month. You're just a few words in a search bar away from the start of a brand new yet very old adventure.

DAY-15

Today, reconnect. In every face-to-face encounter you have, be present. From people at work, to cashiers, to the people in your home, listen fully and make eye contact. Don't rush or interject while they are speaking. This is a lost art, not often seen since before the time of smartphones and the Internet. There is so much more to true connection than just exchanging information via words. Rediscover that presence and you may likely feel conversations deeper and prefer this way of interaction whenever possible. It is, in fact, one of the most beautiful things about being human.

DAY-16

Today, trust yourself more. Your intuition will speak to you as a feeling that you recognize. Getting talked into or talking yourself into going against it will make you doubt your judgment more in the future. Most of the time, you only see the outcome that happens, so if you followed your intuition and second guess yourself later, you've got to trust that the reasons were there but not visible at the time. The more you listen to it, the stronger it will become. If that job, that romance, that friendship, or that purchase doesn't feel right, don't do it. The feeling isn't fear, that's different. The feeling is most clearly described as just not right for you.

DAY-17

Today, decide what are heirlooms and what is trash. Describe three positive things about your mother. Describe three negative things. Describe three positive things about your father. Describe three negative things. What you learned is not who you are, it's just what you learned. Be grateful for those six positive things and pass them down, pass them out, pass them daily into yourself. Become aware of those six negative things as well as their exact opposites. The opposite of too little is too much. In an attempt to get as far away from the pain as possible, you may have gone too far in the other direction, from one extreme to the other. Decide your own middle ground, pass it down, pass it out, and pass it daily into yourself.

DAY-18

Today, add gratitude. To everything. All day. You know when there's a storm and the power goes out for a few hours and how grateful you are when it comes back on? Or when an appliance breaks and then gets fixed a few days later? Or if you've ever had a dream that someone you love passed and it seemed so real but when you wake up, they're just fine and still here? The potential for immense gratitude for so many things and people in your life is always there. Becoming conscious of it and feeling it will create deeper neuronal pathways that serve to elevate your base mood and keep the knowledge alive that whatever annoying or difficult thing life may throw at you, you still have so much to be grateful for.

DAY-19

Today, check your patterns. Whenever you find yourself at the start or in the middle of a familiar pattern that doesn't end well, think about your past decisions. If something happened only once, it could very well have had nothing to do with you. But if it's happened a few times, you likely have had some contribution. And maybe have gone from one extreme to the other. Instead of that, try going with your intuition. Give when it feels good, not when it feels obligated or out of guilt. Speak up when silence hurts, create distance from those who don't value you instead of trying to over do to prove yourself to them. "Go with your heart" means go with what feels good and right to it -- What makes you feel more loved, more confident, and more at peace.

DAY-20

Today, talk yourself through your triggers. Almost everyone has triggers; things that hit nerves of deep pain and throw us into a panicked and disempowered state. They may be financial, or safety-oriented, or have to do with past abuse. They can happen when you get a big bill, are cut off in traffic, or are disrespected in some way. The physical reaction is automatic and immediate, but you can take your power back by consciously becoming aware of when it happens. Breathe deeply. Bring your mind to the present and only the present. Tell yourself that you will get through it, or this isn't worth flipping out over, or to stay calm. You are in full control. We are designed with triggers for survival but the mind, not the body, can decide when a huge reaction isn't needed.

DAY-21

Today, in any area of your life where you are unhappy, write down your options. Take "quitting on yourself" off the table completely. Figure out what is in your power to change. Whether you realize it or not, there are a lot of things that you choose every day. Some are because you want them, some are habit, and others have motivations that only you know inside. A written inventory can help you to see your habits, especially the ones that used to be beneficial but no longer are. Once you become aware of where you can change, you can put your intentions and energy there. "Stuck" may be real, but it may also be a state of mind.

DAY-22

Today, sell yourself on what you want. The fear of disappointment or failure causes most people to sell themselves on what they don't want. So much so that they've given up before they even try. But that is true disappointment and failure. Throughout life, you're going to believe in things and put effort in and it won't always work out. That's just a part of life. It doesn't mean don't bother dreaming and it doesn't mean don't bother making efforts. In the end, you'll know you put your life into what you believed in...whether that's negative or positive is up to you.

DAY-23

Today, daydream. Once something you could get in trouble for, and now you're being told to do it. What? Well, daydreaming when you were supposed to be paying attention to algebra was not the right time or place. But now, or right before you go to bed, is the perfect time. Imagine yourself in great health, having a great time, surrounded by great people who you love or even alone, depending on what you feel like. Imagine your perfect, peaceful life and live in it as a reality in daydreams every single day. It will create a reality in your mind that will help you make decisions more in that direction in your waking life. When that happens, over time, your daydreams will resemble your waking life more and more. Until then, it's a beautiful break; a gift to yourself.

DAY-24

Today, hang in there. Obstacles, setbacks, and things that just about make you want to give up are an inevitable part of life. You may not feel like it, but you are so much stronger than you think. Despair is a horrible state to be in but it happens to everyone, no matter how strong, positive, or responsible you are. Call on your hope and faith and know, please know, there is a way through. If you don't believe it, you'll never find the way but if you do believe it, you will. Believe and then pray, meditate, or both and keep your mind open for answers. They may come in the form of an idea, or asking a friend, or an Internet search or lucky interaction that leads to the miracle that you were looking for. Just please, hang in there.

DAY-25

Today, listen to your body. If you need to rest, rest. If you are feeling run down, you need to take care of you. Withdraw from what or who drains you. Nourish your body with nutritious foods and nourish your mind with positive books and conversations. When your body is barely functioning, everything takes more energy. Take time to renew and recharge your body, mind, and soul.

DAY-26

Today, release a burden. Start with one where you did your best but were not chosen. Whether it was a job, a friendship, or a relationship...change the story that you have been telling yourself. Whether that story was that you weren't good enough or that life isn't fair or that a jerk was chosen over you because nice people finish last...You've got to change the story from within or else its energy will continue to be true for you and will bring you down. Events often only have the meaning we give them. So releasing it could be as simple as saying you weren't chosen because it wasn't right for you but something or someone will be totally right for you in the future.

DAY-27

Today, take an extra minute. Everyone is busy and most of us feel rushed, but take one minute here and there for a hug, or to tell someone you love and appreciate them, or to send someone a message to say hi or check in on someone you care about and haven't heard from in a little while. Even if these minutes only add up to a total of 15 or 20 in a whole day, they may end up being the best and the most valuable and memorable to you and those you love.

DAY-28

Today, look back only to learn and grow. If you look back at the more difficult parts of your past, don't dwell, don't seek to blame, don't relive the pain and anger. Do look back to reflect and retrace your steps and find patterns and your role and responsibility in how they formed. Do this to discover where you need to do things differently from now, on, and to evaluate what caused you to make the choices you made so that you can make better ones in the future. If you don't look back at all, the pattern will likely repeat. If you do learn from the last time, it can truly be the last time, and you can move forward in life with confidence.

DAY-29

Today, listen to understand. If a relationship is important to you, learning how to understand each other is crucial. If an opinion differs on something that matters, it may be that there is a misunderstanding, one person may be reliving a past relationship without realizing it, or an entirely different belief system may be in place. Arguing about who is right or wrong will only lead to division and resentment. Actually listening and understanding each other's point of view with respect that it is true for each in the present moment is the only way to really hear each other and progress to resolve. That is what brings people closer together. Expanding your awareness isn't losing an argument, it's winning peace and a greater depth in your relationship.

DAY-30

Today, make an emergency list. Not flashlights and bread, but your own personal pep talk. Write on a piece of paper 3 times in your life when something you worried and stressed over didn't happen, or didn't happen as awful as you thought. Next, write down 3 times something you hoped for, took a chance, or worked for came through incredibly. Put this list in a safe but accessible place, like tucked away in your wallet. See, when you are down or worried, your mind can get looped in that moment and may even go on a trail of all the times in the past that were similar. That's not helpful and will only get you stuck. This list will serve as your emergency pep talk to remind you of what really is true. When you shift your mindset, you'll be able to see your way through a whole lot easier.

DAY-31

Today, figure out your limitations. Think of things you've put off. Whether it's exercising more, eating better, buying something, cleaning out a closet, going on vacation, starting a business...whatever comes to mind. What is the reason you've put these things off? Usually what will come to mind is lack of something...time, money, motivation. Now take responsibility for and correct it. Lack of time means you find places where you're wasting time. Lack of money means you find ways to spend less or earn more. Lack of motivation means take some first steps because when you start to see results, the motivation will continue. You only ever have "today," and really you only ever have right now. But all your right nows and all your todays will add up so quickly.

DAY-32

Today, actively start looking for the bright side in situations in your life that are challenging you, even if you have to make it up. Straight off, you are going to see things as is -- as bad as or how hard they are. Your bright side may require gratitude at what didn't happen that could have been worse, or confidence in what you will now do in from where you are. Rejected? Be happy single or find someone better. Flat tire? Well maybe if it hadn't gone flat when it did, you'd have had a bad accident just up the road. So what if it's totally made up? There is only one current outcome and to think of your life as would-have-been-better if only something hadn't happened is a made up story, too, but one that makes you feel worse about present day. Instead, tell yourself a story that feels better.

DAY-33

Today, explore. Whether it's your mind, your heart, your neighborhood, local trails or parks, exploring opens your mind and expands your view of the world and of yourself. It challenges you to seek new depths of your soul and heights of your wonder. It keeps your mind active in places that believe in possibilities. Explore for life.

DAY-34

Today, talk back to the voice of doubt in your head. Doubt keeps you small, keeps telling you why you can't, and doesn't care what you want or how you feel. Speak back to it loud and clear with your voice of confidence. Confidence tells you why you can, why you deserve happiness, encourages and believes in you. When one is loud, the other is quiet. Good news is, you get to choose who gets the microphone.

DAY-35

Today, nourish your mind. Make conscious choices of what you are feeding it. Each choice goes in one direction or another; towards health or away from it. At the end of the day, or week, or year, it will all add up. If you want to make a difference, instead of arguing against what you can't stand, use that time to champion for what you love. Support a person you believe in or a charity that is doing good work. Learn something new or do something creative. Your mind, and soul, will thank you.

DAY-36

Today, walk in to your life. When you wake up and all day, look at everything as if it's brand new. Notice all the good things about yourself; who you are and what you have achieved in life. Notice all the good people you've surrounded yourself with. Notice all the things in your life that you have now and once only wished for. Breathe a fresh, new perspective on your life and it will elevate your mind and outlook.

DAY-37

Today, have great conversations. Ones that uplift, teach and learn, and leave you feeling good and fulfilled. There's so much to complain about but there's also so much to enjoy in this world. Reality is a mix of both, even in the hard times.

DAY-38

Today, stop comparing your honest path to the path of someone who is being shady and feeling anger that they are getting away with it. We all choose our own paths and we all end up somewhere that we can't walk back from. While a crooked person may seem a step ahead of you at step 3 or step 100, by the time they reach where they are going it will all crumble. You focus on your path and making it the best it can be. Don't get distracted or start believing you need to be crooked to get anywhere. The end of the road is going to be filled with either gratitude or regret but by then it will be too late to change. You're on the right path, keep going.

DAY-39

Today, make time for yourself. If your first thought was to laugh or say, "yeah right," it's likely you've been subconsciously affirming that you have no time or that you need more time. Beliefs become reality. Once you carve out 5, 10, or 20 minutes per day just for you – where you can take a few deep breaths, have a tea, meditate, read a little, you'll see that you feel better. You'll be more centered and more efficient throughout the day when you give yourself a little space to just be.

DAY-40

Today, appreciate positive contact. Hugs, kind words, giving your dog a scratch behind the ears, or a visit from your cat who wants to sit on your lap for a bit. The loving beings in our lives are never here forever and it's the touch we'll miss one day. Take a little extra time each day to be there, fully present, with everyone you love.

DAY-41

Today, start your day
with three affirmations:

1. Thank you – for waking up this morning to another day of life
2. I am valuable – to center yourself and be able to see when you are and are not being treated as such
3. I am going to make the best of this day – a power thought for all of the expected and unexpected circumstances that present themselves throughout the day.

DAY-42

Today, realize that not everyone thinks the same way you do, and that can be a source of learning. People tend to seek out people who think the same way as they do to feel a comfort in being validated, but it can sometimes be limiting. If you want to be more peaceful, or more confident, or even wealthier, a good thing to do is to listen to someone who is those things already in a positive and authentic way and have an open mind. To be validated is fine, but to learn and grow into a new mindset that you would prefer is more than fine. It's elevating and can help you get unstuck from a place you've always been settling for because you believed it was true...and it was, but only because you truly believed it to be.

DAY-43

Today, find peace where you are. Often when you see inspirational stories, they're told after most or all of the life was lived. About the struggles and the roller coaster until finally the person made it through and was redeemed, rewarded, or validated in some way. But the meantime can sure be a long time. If you live only for the time when the mountain is climbed or the struggle overcome, you'll spend a long time trying, waiting, working, and hoping unhappily. Do your best today and enjoy what and who you do have in your life. Be honest with yourself on if you're being patient or if you're stalling. Course correct. Then, let the rest be. Or at least do your best to let the rest be.

DAY-44

Value your time - literally. You see, people don't value nothing but they do value gifts. Assign a value to your hours. If you do a favor for a friend and they offer you money, either accept it gratefully or decline it by saying, "It's my gift to you." Don't refuse money by saying you don't want it, don't say, "it's nothing," and don't say you'll do something, "for free." It's not free. It's your valuable time; your valuable life. If you choose to do some work without any exchange, it's a valuable gift. Be generous with those who value your time, and selective with those who don't. Give people only as much as they can appreciate.

DAY-45

Today, rewrite your disappointment stories. If you find yourself thinking back to a time when you were disappointed and that is preventing you from doing or trying something now, fast forward a little on that old story. What happened right after the disappointment? You likely learned something, bounced back, and moved on to other things that were good and wouldn't have been in your path had it not been for the disappointment. Now, disappointment isn't ever a good thing, of course. But it's just something that happens in life and usually is not big enough aside from in your mind to prevent you from living, doing, or trying new things that have nothing to do with that old story.

DAY-46

Today, release comparisons to how things "should" be. It's a long time habit that started young...we were just being us and were told to do certain things, be certain ways, not do certain things because if we don't then we'll be in trouble and it will feel bad. So fast forward. If your holiday gathering doesn't remotely resemble the ones in the commercials, or if you're alone or just hanging out with your cat...you don't have to feel bad, or less than, or like you're doing something wrong. Holidays are great for folks who only get together a few times a year and get along well. But for people who don't, you don't have to make it a thing at all. To you, it can be another day, another dinner, no different than the one you had last week. And you can be happy with that.

DAY-47

Today, relax. No, not bubble baths and yoga, unless of course you have time for and want to do that. Relax today in every moment that you remember to do so...like right now. Take a deep breath, let it out and consciously loosen your muscles in your face, neck, and shoulders. Adjust, do a little stretch. Do this often during the day, especially when you start feeling a little tense. It will center you back down to level calm and allow you to make choices and decisions from that good space.

DAY-48

Today, take a step. Something you've always wanted to do, or something you used to do but had to give up for awhile...take a step in that direction. Maybe it's looking up a school, or buying a small thing, even just imagining something in detail. A step opens up a door that can lead to another step, which leads to more. Sooner or later, those steps become a path you've always longed to walk along. Today, take a step.

DAY-49

Today, clarify. If you thought you had some type of agreement but your spouse, friend, boss, or coworker doesn't seem to be following that agreement, take the time to be upfront and clarify. In a non-accusatory way, ask them if you can clarify something; that you were of the understanding that you and they had agreed to a certain thing and you believe you've kept your end but it doesn't seem like they've kept theirs. It could be that they're going through something you don't know about, or that they were absent minded, but until you speak openly with them, you won't know. Don't let things go on unaddressed. That will only lead to resentment and by then today's correctable present will become an uncorrectable past.

DAY-50

Today, respond in a new way. Some people and some situations just push your buttons and can send your mood into a flare almost instantly. Recognize that is a disempowered reaction but that you have a choice instead to make an empowered response. Anything that makes you think, "This always happens to me..." or, "I can't stand it when..." re-evaluate. Because that flare isn't good for you at all. Not physically, not mentally, and not emotionally. Whether you decide the best thing for you is to eliminate the source, create distance from the source, respond differently that before, or accept that's how it is will be up to your discretion. Do what's best for you.

DAY-51

Today, put yourself on the front burner. Of course if you've got minor children or are a primary caregiver, you have to put yourself on the back burner a lot and at any given time. But start making time for and prioritizing yourself. At least put your needs and wants over anyone the breeze blows your way. Help when you genuinely can and genuinely want to, not just when anyone asks. You can be a good person without depleting yourself to the max most of the time.

DAY-52

Today, interrupt yourself and flip the script. A lot of people have a someday "bucket list" for things that they want to do or have that would just take too much time and/or money right now. But there's usually a "can do" smaller experience in a lot of those. You may not be able to take a week at the beach, but you're probably able to go for a ten minute long walk or watch a video online of a beach for five uninterrupted minutes. It's not the vacation or break you really want, but it's one you can do today. Live and experience and enjoy them fully while you're in them, no matter how brief they are. Look for other can dos in your daily life and give yourself a little taste of all you want. It does make a difference to your overall wellbeing.

DAY-53

Today, become aware of your motivations. They all boil down to one of two; love or fear. The more choices you make from love, the better and more fulfilled your paths will be. This goes for what you read, who you engage with, why you give, and what you commit to. Becoming aware means to pause and ask yourself, "Why am I really doing (or not doing) this?" throughout the day. Is it because you want to, because you are afraid someone will be mad if you don't, because it triggered a reaction in you, because you will look forward to it...you may surprise yourself with your responses. If they are mostly out of fear, start a journal and jot down notes to change the habits if there are some that you want and are ready to change.

DAY-54

Today, realize that there is no one big mountain to climb and then it's all smooth sailing from there. If you're holding your breath and exhausting yourself trying to reach what you think will be the happily ever after point, you'll be spent and won't have enjoyed much when you get there and realize there's more ahead. Enjoy what you can about each day. Prioritize what needs to be done as goals but don't let them consume your every waking moment with worry. Health, money, and relationship challenges may all pile on you at once and feel overwhelming. Put your health first. Without that, none of the other things will be done well. Others may not understand but you can't allow yourself to be run over just so they have a smoother ride.

DAY-55

Today, forgive someone who you already no longer speak with...fully. So that next time they come to mind, you won't have any reaction or charge or urge to retell one of the old battle stories. You'll just think, "Oh wait, I've accepted that happened and it no longer affects me." It really is a choice. It really is that simple, and you won't believe how empowering and freeing it really is, too.

DAY-56

Today, realize that knowing you have value doesn't make you conceited, just as you valuing someone else who is a good person is a good thing, too. Knowing you have value means that you have love, appreciation, and care for yourself. When you do this, you'll become immune to those who do not truly care for, appreciate, or have genuine love for you. This is why it's so necessary to feel and recognize it from within.

DAY-57

Today, start to consciously heal your triggers. Triggers are situations, either real or projected, that cause you to overreact...just like how pulling a small trigger on a gun causes a big explosion. They are usually leftovers from childhood and make you feel powerless. Become aware of them and affirm their opposites. For example, if you blow up when someone wastes your time, affirm, "I spend my time wisely." You will lose attraction to time wasters. Replace "I can't stand when someone takes me for granted" with, "I am valued and appreciated." If you believe in or fear something, you draw it to you. Become empowered by changing beliefs and they will no longer be drawn into your reality. This won't all happen immediately, but it will happen with practice and time.

DAY-58

Today, realize that you will fail in life. Accept it. It's part of life that not one single person ever escapes. Once you accept it, you won't have to fear it so much anymore. People often do what they think is safe to avoid failure...or listen to sensible words of well meaning other people. But failing at what you really want and believe in isn't nearly as disappointing as failure or even succeeding at what you have little passion for if any at all. And the one thing about failure is, it's pretty much always a learning step along the way to success. It's not an end but a redirection along the path you are creating as you sculpt your unique and amazing life.

DAY-59

Today, develop a love for learning that which you're already interested in. There are some things that you have no interest in learning and really don't have to. But other things, that you have an interest in or are curious about, don't let the fact that you don't know much yet deter you from learning. Learning is usually the most difficult only in the beginning until you get the basics down. Then, you become free to be creative and your mind will bloom into them. Learning when we were young often involved "having to" in school and a lot of people associated learning with being forced and not fun at all. But there's also a feeling of achievement in learning things that you want to learn that isn't found anywhere else. It gives a unique form of satisfaction and peace.

DAY-60

Today, affirm that you have time. Affirmations are repeated statements that reshape beliefs. Beliefs create reality -- whether you are conscious of them or not. If you've been repeating that you are always busy and never have time, those affirmations have cemented themselves by now. There's always more that needs doing. You constantly feel rushed and remember 20 more things as you try to sleep. Start some new affirmations. "I always have more than enough time." "I have time for myself." At first, this will seem so not true. But keep at it, especially when you face situations where you'd normally panic. Things will shift. You will start to see changes in your reality. You will be able to breathe and feel in control of how you manage your life. Just give it a little time.

DAY-61

Today, practice observation. Of course it's good to speak up and speak your mind when it's important, but there's a lot to be learned from observation and listening, too. Things can get complicated and run off on tangents when people interrupt each other to try and be heard. Sometimes when you take a step back and observe, you can better see when something isn't about you or some small issue at all, but rather something that someone is battling within themselves and hasn't quite figured out yet. To jump in defensively would only recreate the outer role they think they need to fight. You can choose not to fulfill that.

DAY-62

Today, stop calling anything that didn't work out a failure. If you believed in something, if you invested your time and effort with good intentions, there's no failure there. Some things work for awhile and then don't, some things were doomed from the start but you didn't realize it right away, and some things run their course and the course turns out to be less than forever. You can either look back and see a bunch of failures in your past or you can see a bunch of experiences. How you view yourself, your present, and your future is going to be affected by what you call them and what you believe them to be. It's really hard to be motivated if you think all you've done is failed, but a lot easier when you realized you've lived, loved, tried, believed, and learned.

DAY-63

Today, reflect on your path. Think back to who you were 10, 20, or however many years ago you left childhood and went out into the world. Now just for a moment, think about how well you've done in life; whether that means making it big or even just accomplishing the arrival to today...either way, your much younger self would be so impressed. In this world where products are sold often on the guise of poking at people feeling they are lacking something or are not enough, just recognize for a moment your journey to this point and all that you have gone through to get here. Give yourself some credit and gratitude for who you are today.

DAY-64

Today, become aware of if you're in a pit. If you are, it's not usually because you leaped in willingly – more likely you were pushed. Others can help you get out, but only if you choose to and only if you reach out your hand. Or, you may need to climb out on your own which will take time and focused effort. Some people lament about the push or the fall and while it's good to know how you got there so you can avoid repeating it in the future, it's not the way out. You've got to remember who you are. Find your resilience. Have faith that you'll be on level ground again and put your best, most positive thoughts and affirmations into getting there. You could justifiably remain stuck and it wasn't fair and it wasn't your fault. But if that's not the life you want to live, start climbing out.

DAY-65

Today, set goal intentions for your day. Not every day can be the same, nor should it be. If it's a day that you are working, goal intentions may be, "Today, I will be productive and at peace." If you have a day ahead of an outing, shopping, a day of cleaning, or one of unwinding, setting goal intentions can help you to be fully in the space you are in during the time you are there and feeling accomplished afterward. When you make time to relax, relax. When you make time to have fun, have fun. When you make time to work, work. Each has an important role in balance and overall satisfaction with life.

DAY-66

Today, create a three phase goal; daily, monthly, and five years. Whether it be health, finances, learning, or the first thing that came to your mind that has maybe always been in the back of it. An example could be health. A 5 year goal is to be healthier than today. A monthly goal is to eat healthier foods. A daily goal is to add some kind of exercise time....a ten minute walk or 15 minute exercise video from YouTube. When you take care of the days and months, the long term adds up. Start today. Start with reasonable changes that you can stick with. You can increase them later if you like. There is no trick or shortcut to the big long-term goal. It's just cumulative of what you do each day.

DAY-67

Today, release and replace. Some bad thought about yourself or someone else that finds its way into your mind each day...sometimes many times each day. Release it by replacing it. For example, if you often call yourself a name when you make a mistake or get something wrong or forget something, don't carry that thought through. Replace it with an opposite...something you're good at or something you can find some gratitude for yourself for. If it's a thought about someone else...stirring up old hurts or thinking to blame someone who's gone for circumstances that remain, replace those with present day things you can be grateful for instead. Rewire your reactions and your whole view of life will change.

DAY-68

Today, choose motivations from a level up than the one you are at now. Opening back up after pain, heartbreak, illness, financial hard times, or loss can be anxiety-ridden if not terrifying. But to get back to "you," at least consider what your choices would be "if." If you were healthier, or wealthier, or more confident, or if your trust were still intact. Often, people only consider the reality of now versus perfection and end up feeling deflated. If you were at the bottom of a mountain and only thought of there versus the top, it would seem like an impossible climb. Instead, just imagine if you were one step higher and summon up some courage and take that step. You may not get to the top, but if you take those steps, the view will get better and better.

DAY-69

Today, begin with a clean slate, even if only in your mind. To your mind, imagination is the same as reality, which is why your adrenaline can be set off by a noise at night whether that noise was an intruder or a playful kitten. So today, start with an intention to clear all debt, whether it's money owed, money borrowed, or emotional debts like regret or resentment. Announce in your mind that all debt, inward and outward, is forgiven. If you do this sufficiently with true belief, you will become open to opportunities to make it true in real life and will close off to circumstances that would make it false. Belief drives reality and you can consciously choose your beliefs.

DAY-70

Today, realize when an argument about a little thing isn't about the little thing at all. If you think it's about the little thing, their – or your -- reaction may seem blown way out of proportion. But if you realize the little thing is a last straw, just the tip of the iceberg on miles deep pain of not feeling enough, not feeling valued, not feeling safe, or not feeling loved, you can skip being distracted by how insignificant the little thing is and focus on healing the larger issue at hand.

DAY-71

Today, connect with your breath. Every time you think of it during the day, take one deep breath. Inhale and exhale slowly and comfortably deep, on a count in of three and a count out of three. What's the point of something so simple? It connects you fully to now and centers you in your body. You'll be less likely to get distracted or caught up in some type of over thinking about the past or anxiety about the future. Conscious breathing is an ancient art, but not many people were ever taught it. It's free, easy, and you can start right now. You'll feel different by the end of the day, less on edge. Doing this every day will lead to longer lasting improvements as well.

DAY-72

Today, realize that "going with the flow" may not always be the best idea. The goal of it seems fine, keep the peace and don't cause any disruption. But who is in charge of the direction? Is it the strongest, most considerate person in the group, or the loudest, most erratic, self-centered, and dramatic? If it's the latter, it's probably taken you on many trips that were fraught with unnecessary pain and conflict. If that's the case, it may be time for you to either take charge or jump ship. Start your own flow and go with that.

DAY-73

Today, create and put out a new, positive belief about yourself. Something about you personally like, "I always figure new things out quickly." Or something about how you interact with the world like, "The roads are always clear when I drive." Ones about yourself will create subconscious confidence, and ones about the world will create a new subconscious choice system of where to put your attention, where and when to act, and what to focus on. Remember, belief drives reality. If you want your reality to change, seed it with new, positive beliefs.

DAY-74

Today, start to believe things are easier than they appear. Come back out of your shell. Now, if you've been going through some really tough times lately, your first reaction to that statement may be very angry and that's understandable. Having to just try and survive for a long time doesn't result in the happiest of moods. But honestly and from experience, change does come from the inside and there are times when you're crouched down still clinging to the umbrella but the bulk of the storm has passed and you already made it through. It's not until you realize it that you can begin to breathe easier, put down the umbrella, and start to enjoy the sunshine again.

DAY-75

Today, realize and recognize this truth: You don't know in advance how anything is going to turn out for sure. All you know is what your choices and actions are, your reasons for them, and the information you know in the beginning and along the way. So as long as you are doing your best, doing what you believe is right, being honest and straightforward, and staying aware of information that comes to you...you're doing your part to ensure that things go well. If they don't: by chance, accident, or even deception, you can't regret what you couldn't possibly have foreseen. But if they turn out wonderfully, you've earned that result by who you chose to be. Live well.

DAY-76

Today, start to figure out what you want in life. Look at it like ordering from a menu. You decide what you want, then choose it, speaking clearly. If it's sold out, you choose something else. If they bring you something you didn't order, you can decide to keep it or refuse it. If you went to a restaurant and asked them to bring you "whatever," odds are that it would be what other people like, but it may not be for you. You decide. You choose. You ask. Stop thinking it's selfish or inconsiderate to make your needs known. Needs can be modest, fair, or demanding. Only demanding ones put others out. So don't be demanding but be honest about your needs. You can't really feel cared about by the people around you and grateful for them if your needs always go unmet.

DAY-77

Today, be able to say "no" without first saying "sorry." Be able to express your opinion without first saying "sorry." Sorry is for regrets, things you've done wrong, either by accident or on purpose. Sorry is for condolences. Sorry is not for apologizing for who you are - a good person with valid needs and opinions, too.

DAY-78

Today, give yourself peace. Take three deep breaths. Close your eyes and think of three things; material, people, or pets, that are in your life right now that you feel gratitude for. Imagine each one and continue to breathe deeply, filling your heart space with appreciation. Relax your neck, shoulders, face, and enjoy this peace.

DAY-79

Today, remember that you are a part of nature and are like nature. Tides go up and down, so do moods. Riverbeds dry up and others form elsewhere, so do your opportunities. Leaves fall, but then buds form and new leaves and flowers emerge. So do your relationships. You are not your low tides, dried up riverbeds, and fallen leaves. Those can feel painful and difficult but they are just part of your unfolding, evolving lifetime.

DAY-80

Today, become aware of all that you've been carrying for years that weighs you down. Doubt, fears, failures, heartbreaks, loss, and anything that shrinks you and dims your light. The day you decide you're going to set it all down may not feel remarkable at first. But as you go on, in every day, consciously choosing to do it again and again, you will start to breathe easier. You will react less to things that remind you of that old pain because you have chosen to respond differently. You will radiate happiness for no particular reason. You will become more and more free...free to be you.

Congratulations!

You did it. You made it to the end of 80 days. Think back to who you were at the start and all you've learned about yourself along the way. So here you are now. Opened up, enlightened, more free, and more at peace. And you've done it all in such a short time but it was the conscious effort, persistence, and honesty that you brought to it that made it happen. Continue with this commitment to knowing and developing your true self. Your life will continue to bloom, brighten, and grow in so many beautiful ways.

LET'S KEEP IN TOUCH!

www.HappinessinYourLife.com

www.theHiYL.com

FB/Happinessinyourlife

Instagram: @happinessinyourlife

Made in the USA
Las Vegas, NV
31 March 2021